Caernarfon
Through the Eye of Time

This book is dedicated to two of the author's closest friends who came to his aid in his hour of need on more than one occasion: to Ms Christine Taylor of Caernarfon especially for her expertise in preparing the text ready for the publishers, and to Mr Gareth Edwards also of Caernarfon, for enhancing old photos and ensuring that they were suitable for reproduction.

Caernarfon
Through the Eye of Time

T. Meirion Hughes

First impression: 2014

© Copyright T. Meirion Hughes and Y Lolfa Cyf., 2014

Cover design: Y Lolfa
Cover photograph: J. J. Dodd

ISBN: 978 184771 930 0

Published and printed in Wales
on paper from well-maintained forests by
Y Lolfa Cyf., Talybont, Ceredigion SY24 5HE
website www.ylolfa.com
e-mail ylolfa@ylolfa.com
tel 01970 832 304
fax 832 782

Contents

Foreword

Most weekday mornings Meirion Hughes may be seen on the corner of Y Maes, a tall man, taller by a head than most around him. He is talking, listening, doing what generations of Caernarfon's people have done in that particular place, sharing the news, keeping the necessary legends alive.

Some of the pieces in this book are familiar, but often Meirion introduces precious new details between the lines of the old mosaic. I shall mention three examples.

The Caernarfon Pavilion was a large building with a seating capacity of 8,000, built in 1877, a testament to the confidence of Welsh Nonconformity. The building was the cultural and political arena for Gwynedd and beyond. The acoustics were good and remained so down the years, the silver flattering tones of David Lloyd George, the local M.P., the rounded notes of Paul Robeson the American bass who loved Wales, the united voices of the many good choirs singing for so many good causes, were all heard here during the 80 years of the Pavilion's golden age.

I found particular pleasure in the unofficial census taken by Meirion Hughes and friends one fine Saturday night in the summer of 1949. By 1949 the local buses were popular and necessary – between the decline of the railways and the supremacy of the family saloon car. On Saturdays fleets of these buses filled the roads converging on Caernarfon, bringing the population of the hinterland to the town to meet, drink, eat and talk in milkbars, cinemas and public parks. Meirion Hughes and some friends decided to take an unofficial census and they counted 78 coaches and double-deckers leaving the town between 9 and 10 p.m. on that wondrous summer's night, a total of some few thousand Welsh speakers living the dream. Caernarfon was the gleaming gem in a precious necklace of villages from Y Felinheli on the sea shore to the east, up to Deiniolen at a thousand feet above sea level and then from Llanberis and Llanrug along the slate country down the Nantlle valley to the pastoral fields of Llanwnda and Llandwrog. Meirion has recorded a segment of our cultural history.

One chapter devoted to the adventurous Lionel Wilmot Brabazon Rees is poignant and timely as we prepare to remember the First World War. Lionel Rees was the last of the Rees publishing dynasty in the town, his grandfather had founded *Yr Herald Cymraeg* in 1855 – probably the most successful of all Welsh newspapers. The grandson chose a different career from printing and publishing and enrolled as a pilot in the old R.F.C. and became a hero above the fields of the Flanders and Northern France. He was much decorated wearing the VC and the MC with pride.

Lionel Rees was a solitary hero in the air and on the sea who single-handedly sailed his twelve ton yacht from Caernarfon to the Bahamas in 1933. He married a native girl and lived and died there with his family so very far from Caernarfon. Lionel Rees will surely be remembered during the centenary commemorations of the Great War.

This book is often a treasure chest of the purest gold. Diolch i chi Meirion am rannu'r trysorau efo ni.

R. Maldwyn Thomas
Bangor
April 2014

Appreciation

At this time last year my Welsh language book *Hanesion Tre'r Cofis* was launched and was well received. Consequently I was asked by Mr Lefi Gruffudd of Y Lolfa publishers to consider writing an English version of the book for the benefit of non-Welsh readers and *Caernarfon through the Eye of Time* became my new challenge as is the writing of any book.

No-one can achieve such a task without the aid of a team, and the author can only be part of the team. Therefore my wholehearted thanks go to the following persons:

Mr R. Maldwyn Thomas and Dr Glenda Carr, both related and former pupils of the old Grammar School in Caernarfon. They are well-known for their literary achievements in the Welsh language circles;

Mr Glyn Tomos, who is the chairman of the editorial committee of the community paper *Papur Dre* and has worked closely with me for over a decade;

Ms Christine Taylor who prepared the text ready for the publishers;

Mr Gareth Edwards of the Caernarfon Online Website for enhancing the old photographs thus making them suitable for a high standard of reproduction;

The staff of the Gwynedd Archives Service at Caernarfon for their assistance when researching and also fellow researchers:

Miss Norah Davies of the Gwynedd Family History Society.

Mr Keith Morris, Caernarfon Traders website.

Mr Geraint Roberts, military researcher.

Others that I owe a debt of gratitude to are mentioned in the articles themselves.

Finally many thanks to Mr Lefi Gruffudd and the staff at Y Lolfa for producing another attractive volume on the historic town of Caernarfon.

Sincerely,
T. Meirion Hughes
April 2014

King of Captains

During the 19th century, when Caernarfon was a busy slate-exporting port, many of its sons embarked on a career as seafarers and some became master mariners of repute. However, none of them ever enjoyed the success of the son of a coachman, born on 13 August 1845, in no. 23 Pool Hill.

According to the Census of 1851, Griffith and Margaret Pritchard had four children, three daughters and one son, John. He was their second child and was educated at the old National School (Yr Ysgol Rad) in the early 1850s. Mr Foster was the headmaster and had held the post since the school was opened in 1843. He received further instruction in navigation from Captain Robert Morris, a retired master mariner who kept a school in Pool Side, and went to sea at the age of 13 in 1858.

His first ship was the 117 tonne Caernarfon schooner *Empress*, his master and owner being Captain Thomas Hudson, the maternal grandfather of the well-known Welsh scholar and Caernarfon-born Professor T. Hudson Williams, author of the book *Atgofion am Gaernarfon* (Memories of Caernarfon), 1950.

In 1860, young John joined the crew of the new 120 tonne schooner *Eleanor Thomas*, whose master and owner was William Thomas, better remembered as the first captain of the well-known Caernarfon-built schooner *Napoleon*. It was extremely fortunate that he did, for the *Empress* was lost with all hands off Hamburg in 1860.

John Pritchard worked hard at his studies and in 1868 he qualified for his second mate's certificate. In 1870 he was again successful in attaining his first mate's certificate and at the age of 29, he passed his final exams for master mariner. It was not long before he had command of a ship and it is known that he became master of two vessels: the *Prince of Wales* and the *Sybil Wynn*.

During this period he married the sister of D. T. Edwards, licensee of the Drum Inn, Market Street, and both he and his brother-in-law had shares in the *Sybil Wynne*. In 1879, he left Caernarfon and the next reference to him states that he had been given the task of bringing out a new 80 tonne steamer *Princess of Wales* from the shipyard at Wallsend on the Tyne, and this is believed to be the smallest steamer ever to have been built.

Shortly afterwards he joined the Cunard Shipping Company and served for 14 years as mate on several of the larger passenger ships. In 1894 the opportunity arose for him to be given the command of the *Samaria* and from then on, until his retirement in 1910, he was captain of at least a dozen of the company's largest vessels, such as the *Carmania*, *Caronia*, *Campania*, *Etruria*, *Lucania* and *Saxonia*.

In 1907, he was summoned once again to Wallsend to take charge of the latest and best-known in her day, Cunard's liner *Mauretania*. This steamer was 331 times heavier than the *Princess of Wales* which he had safely brought out of Wallsend 28 years previously.

It is indeed difficult to imagine the size of this giant liner, which needed over 800 staff that included 70 sailors, 366 engineers and 376 stewards to be responsible for the comfort and well-being of the passengers, 812 in all. Only one of them had overall charge of the others, Captain John Pritchard from Pool Hill, Caernarfon, who went to sea as a cabin boy at the age of 13, nearly half a century earlier.

During the 30 years that he was employed by Cunard, he was commended twice. The first time was in 1881 when he was a mate on the *Samaria*. Whilst crossing the Atlantic, a schooner from Wales was found to be in difficulties and on the verge of sinking. The Captain placed John Pritchard in charge of a lifeboat which was sent to assist, and despite the rough weather and the risk involved, all members of the schooner's crew were saved. For this act of bravery, John Pritchard received the silver medal of the Royal Humane Society. His second commendation came in 1908, when, as captain of the *Mauretania*, he was on the homeward bound journey from New York and learned that an American barque was in difficulties. He immediately gave orders to change course and sailed to the crew's assistance. When President Roosevelt learned of what the captain of the world's largest vessel had done, he gave orders to the American Consul in Liverpool to present him with a pair of binoculars and a certificate acknowledging yet another humane act. His master's certificate was also stamped with the seal of the American Board of Trade with the words 'Certified that a Binocular Glass was presented by the American Government to John Pritchard in recognition of services rendered in rescuing the crew of the American Barque *Falls River*, 3 January 1908'.

On a return voyage from New York in 1907, he again made history. A new channel had been dug seven miles long, to enable the harbour to accommodate larger liners and at the same time cut five miles off the journey. It was the *Caronia* in the charge of Captain Pritchard that had the honour of being the first ship to negotiate the New Ambrose Channel, as it was called.

Despite being in the limelight, he was a very modest man. When the *Mauretania* arrived in New York on her maiden voyage, the harbour was swarming with newspapermen and they all wished to interview the Captain, but he refused to be interviewed and reminded them of his responsibilities and of how busy he was.

R.M.S. Mauretania

Captain Pritchard
on board the
Mauretania

However, one reporter, more persistent than the others, appealed to him: 'Captain Pritchard from Caernarfon, North Wales, the American public are anxious to hear from you. Can you say something that they will appreciate?' His immediate reply was 'You can tell them that I have worked for the Cunard Line for nearly 30 years and that the cap I wore then still fits me'. The reporter had sufficient material for his article and the following morning all the papers had many column inches on the arrival of the *Mauretania* under such headings as 'Some Captain, some ship'.

In January 1909, 18 months after the Mauretania's maiden voyage, John Pritchard received the highest honour that the Cunard Line could bestow upon him. He was promoted Commodore of the Fleet, which meant that the *Mauretania* was allowed to fly a little swallow tailed flag, embellished with the crest of the line, an honour reserved for the Fleet's Commodore.

The lad from Caernarfon was then 63 years old and one would have expected that he had reached the pinnacle of his career, but there was one honour yet to come. In September 1909 the *Mauretania* broke the record for crossing the Atlantic at an average speed of 26.06 knots per hour, a record which would stand until 1929, seven years after the death of Captain Pritchard.

He retired in 1910 and died at Meols, Cheshire on

29 January 1922, aged 76. The *Caernarfon and Denbigh Herald* published an account of the funeral, which was held on 3 February, stating that the chief mourner was his son, Captain William G. Pritchard. A large contingent of the maritime fraternity, including several high-ranking officials of the Cunard Line attended and the internment was at West Derby cemetery. Among the floral tributes was a wreath from his second wife and his stepsons, Leonard and Keith.

John Pritchard was indeed a remarkable man and can justly be referred to as the *Herald* put it, 'King of Captains'.

A Hero at 19

One wonders how many Gwynedd people are aware of the history of a young man who received his early education at the Boys' School, South Penrallt, Caernarfon. His photograph can be seen above marked by a cross in the front row of class 3A in the year 1930/31. A copy of the photo was given to me by Mr Tom Glyn Griffiths (he is the fifth from the left in the middle row) and we can all be extremely grateful to him for bringing to our notice that which happened in the middle of the Atlantic on Guy Fawkes Day in the year 1940.

John Lewis Jones lived with his parents and

brother, Leonard, in Wynne Street, Caernarfon in the early 1930s and, according to Tom Griffiths, he was a promising artist in his early years. His father was a member of the police force and was posted to Nefyn in the mid 1930s and the family settled down there, John Lewis having to leave the Caernarfon Grammar School and attend a Pwllheli school.

At the age of 16, in the year 1937, he decided on a career in the Merchant Navy and joined his first ship, a tanker named *San Felix* as an apprentice in navigation. That ship became his home for nine and a half months as she transported oil from the Dutch East Indies, visiting ports such as Rio de Janeiro, Montevideo and Buenos Aires. Then in 1938, John joined another tanker named the *San Demetrio* and, according to his own testimony, he learnt more about the work during the next 21 months than he would have normally. He was on this ship when World War II broke out on 3 September 1939, and from then on, as in the case of many other young men, his training intensified and he had to take on responsibilities far sooner than had it been in peace time.

The *San Demetrio* was in a convoy of ships escorted by the British Destroyer *HMS Jervis Bay* and at 4.30 p.m. on the afternoon of 5 November 1940, they were attacked by the German Battleship *Admiral von*

Scheer. Although the *Jervis Bay* fought very bravely there was little she could do against the fire power of the larger ship. The battleship then attacked the merchant ships at will, thus creating havoc. The *San Demetrio* was struck several times by the guns of the *Admiral von Scheer* and she caught fire. It was then, at 5.30 p.m., that Captain Waite gave the order to abandon ship and make for the lifeboats. Jack Lewis, as he was called in the Boys' School, found himself on one of the lifeboats and, as one of the boats could not be launched due to it being full of water, the second officer and his crew joined them. They observed another boat with the first officer-in-charge. He had been given instructions to row as quickly as possible away from the *San Demetrio* lest she should explode. Jack Lewis' crew did likewise, but by then they had lost contact with the other lifeboat.

Sometime during the afternoon of the following day, 6 November, a ship was sighted on the horizon and the lifeboat set sail in her direction. As it drew near it became apparent that the ship was the *San Demetrio*, but due to the rough sea it was not possible to board her. The following day, however, the sea was a bit calmer and they succeeded in doing so. The ship was still on fire and all the crew worked exceedingly hard to extinguish it. The next day it was decided that the priority would be to attempt

The *San Demetrio*

to get the engines in working order and the chief engineer and three volunteers, one of whom was the apprentice, John Lewis Jones, risked their lives to go down below, where there were toxic gases that could have overcome them at any time, and there they remained for some considerable time, opening valves and attending to the boilers.

During that same afternoon, the chief engineer announced that the engines could then be restarted, but they had no means of navigating the ship, due to the compasses having been damaged by the fire. They then had to make a decision as to whether to return in the direction of North America or to continue on an easterly course for home. The weather report, however, was eventually the deciding factor, bad weather being expected to the west.

Jack Lewis took his turn at the wheel alternately with the chief engineer and they relied upon the sun during the day and the stars at night to guide them towards Europe. On 13 November they sighted land on the horizon, but that which caused them concern was the location. Was it Ireland, a neutral country, or was it the coast of occupied France? Fortunately, it proved to be the former – a bay on the west coast of Ireland. From there they were escorted by a naval warship all the way to Greenock on the Clyde where a tremendous welcome awaited them. The chief engineer and his small crew had succeeded in repairing the pumps and the cargo of 11,000 tons of oil was safely discharged, with only 200 tons having been lost due to the damage.

Several members of the crew, including the chief engineer, Charles Pollard, and the apprentice, John Lewis Jones, were duly honoured for their bravery. Both of them received the Lloyds War Medal for valour and on 21 February 1941, less than four months after the attack by the *Admiral von Scheer*, the apprentice, John Lewis Jones, was awarded the BEM. In addition to this, all those who had taken part in the reboarding of the *San Demetrio* after the attack, received a share of the salvage money of £14,000 for their part in safeguarding the cargo.

As a result of this remarkable episode in the history of Word War II, a film called *San Demetrio*

John (Jack)
Lewis Jones

London was produced by Ealing Studios in 1943 and is still available to buy.

The ship was repaired and was back in service for some months afterwards. However, on St Patrick's Day, 1942, it was sunk by a torpedo fired from a German submarine the *U404* and all 48 lives on board were lost.

Fortunately, at that time, John Lewis Jones was serving on another ship and survived the War. He remained in the Merchant Navy, sat the appropriate examinations and ended his career as a Captain. He was, however, forced to retire through ill health at the age of 50, in 1971. He returned to Nefyn where he spent the rest of his days in retirement and took an active interest in the Porthdinllaen lifeboat and spent much time painting, his childhood hobby. He died in 1986, aged 65.

The *Hindoo*

No! I shall not discuss one of the religions of the world on this occasion, but a ship that was registered in the port of Caernarfon. Her owner was no less a person than Humphrey Owen, Rhyddgaer, Llanidan, Anglesey, who became more well-known as the owner of the Vulcan Foundry in Victoria Dock, Caernarfon.

Two centuries ago, earning a living in north Wales had become so difficult that many families had to pack their bags and leave the land of their birth in the hope of meeting with better opportunities on the other side of the Atlantic. Emigrating was a dangerous business in the 18th and 19th centuries, many risking their lives and that of their families on sailing ships unsuitable for crossing the ocean on a journey which could take from three to six months. On occasions, almost half the passengers would lose their lives before reaching the coast of America. This happened in the mid 18th century in the history of one of our best-known poets, Goronwy Owen from Anglesey. He lost his wife and child on the voyage.

But, by the end of the 1830s things had improved. A three-masted barque was built in the Merigomish district of Picton, Nova Scotia, in 1838, and her owners at that time were George Macleod (ship builder), Richard Jones (merchant, Holyhead) and Humphrey Owen. She was registered as the *Hindoo* in Beaumaris on 12 June 1839. Later she was re-registered in Caernarfon as a 380 ton barque to carry 400 passengers, and a crew of 15 was required to sail her. From 1840 to 1847 her captain was Richard Hughes, and it is believed that she safely crossed the Atlantic 25 times there and back during that period. This is equivalent to three return journeys per annum and on one occasion completed the voyage in two months and 20 days.

She was a Caernarfon ship for 21 years between

1840 and 1861, before she was sold to Liverpool. As a result many hundreds of Welsh-speaking Welshmen from Anglesey, Meirioneth, Caernarfon and Denbigh sailed on her to the USA to start a new life.

Poverty had forced them to leave their country and to sail to the other end of the world, where they believed it would be easier for them to earn a living, where there would be better opportunities for their children, without ever considering returning to Wales or to see the loved ones they left behind again. They all had a one-way ticket.

Richard Hughes' time as her captain was the one that brought fame to her as a passenger ship and the late Welsh historian Bob Owen, Croesor, in an article on the *Hindoo*, relates the story of a huge storm on the ocean that lasted for four days. Many of the passengers suffered from seasickness and others had given up all hope of ever seeing land again. It occurred in April 1842 and one person, Edward Rees of Llanegryn, Meirioneth, went to the captain and asked him for permission to hold a prayer meeting. The captain agreed and Edward Rees gathered a number of regular worshippers from amongst the passengers and entered these words in his diary: 'Went to the Cabin and Griffith Roberts, Clynnog, fell on his knees and started to pray. It was 5 p.m. and by 9 p.m. not a gust of wind could be heard'.

This, gives us today, an idea of what kind of people

many of those who emigrated were. People from a religious background who just wished to improve their living conditions and start a new life where they would be free to worship without fear of landowners persecuting them for being nonconformists.

Captain Richard Hughes was himself of the same nature and deserved all praise that the passengers and crew all reached New York safely in 42 days despite the elements. The Captain took command of another ship owned by Humphrey Owen named *Higginson* in 1847 and again crossed the Atlantic in her many times loaded with passengers, but by 1852 he became captain of a ship called *Jane* from Beaumaris. In a Welsh American newspaper, *Y Cenhadwr Americanaidd* he is described as an experienced sailor and master mariner '...who once was master of the *Higginson* of Caernarfon and had completed 25 return journeys to America in the vessel *Hindoo* and in all these voyages he never lost a bolt or a sail, but merely 'one stencil boom'. He always sailed without alcoholic spirits, other than a small amount for medicinal purposes.

On one occasion, however, the *Hindoo* got into difficulties on arriving at the USA and was accused of carrying more immigrants than was legally allowed. The evidence of what happened is scanty, but according to one source, the company had to pay $150 per head for 90 passengers who were over the limit of the 150 allowed, even though the majority of them were children.

By 1853 steam ships had become far more popular with travellers and there was less call for sailing ships like the *Hindoo* due to their being faster and more comfortable. In the year 1861, the *Hindoo* was sold to Liverpool, putting an end to her connection with the port of Caernarfon. Her importance in the history of the town lies in the fact that she was a truly Welsh ship with a crew of Welsh sailors, and very many Welsh speakers from north-west Wales emigrated to North America by means of this ship. It's estimated that during the 21 years the *Hindoo* was registered in Caernarfon she crossed the Atlantic, both ways, 60 times and carried a total of some thousands intending to settle in the 'land of milk and honey'.

There's no doubt that she was considered by everyone in Caernarfon as 'The *Hindoo* from Caernarfon'.

Here is a translation of what a Welsh poet said about the *Hindoo*:

The golden crown of Caernarfon
Is the *Hindoo* riding the waves.

An Old Caernarfon Family

It is hardly likely that anyone who has lived in Caernarfon for any length of time will not have heard of this family and associate it with the age of the Caernarfon schooners and the activities on the waterfront, during the 19th century. One need only mention the name Aber, Porth yr Aur and the surname Pritchard, and almost everyone living in the area will have guessed as to whom I refer. Yes, the family of Dafydd 'R Aber, as it is known to all in Caernarfon. Needless to say the name is far older than anyone today can remember, but how old? That is the question.

One has to search through the Census returns of the mid 19th century to trace the first David Pritchard whose name is associated with transporting passengers across the mouth of the river Seiont. The Census of 1851 shows David Pritchard to be a seaman, married to Sarah (aged 22, born in Dartford, Kent) and they had one daughter, Emma, twelve months old and living at no. 7, Shirehall Street (Stryd y Jêl). However, on the 1861 Census, David or Dafydd had left the sea and was a boatman or ferryman on the Aber or Coed Helen Ferry and by then had three children, Emma, aged twelve, David C. aged ten and John B. Pritchard, aged four. In 1864, however, Emma died and was buried in Llanfaglan Church cemetery. According to the Census of 1871, David Pritchard was still the boatman and with his eldest son David C. (aged 19) assisting him and his youngest son John B., aged 13, still at school. In the 1881 Census David Pritchard is described as boat owner and David C. as being an employee of his while John B's name is not recorded. The father died in 1884 (aged 76), and the 1891 Census shows David C. Pritchard to be the boat owner, his brother John B. as his assistant and a young lad, Griffith Evans (age 16), as a boat boy for them.

It is more than likely that this was the situation when the Caernarfon Borough Council decided to build the first Aber bridge, which was officially opened on St David's Day, 1900. This meant that the Council would, according to law, have had to pay compensation to the owner of the ferry. While the actual figure that David Charles Pritchard received is not known, it is believed to have been a considerable sum as he was able to buy a bakery at Bryngwyn, Llanrug and he and his wife then moved there to live. It was where his first son, David Charles Pritchard, the same name as his father, was born and his name appears on the Census of 1901 as being aged seven months. On the same Census the father was said to be 'living on his means'.

Again there is no evidence to show how long he enjoyed living under those circumstances, but in 1908 he put his property, Bryngwyn Bach, Llanrug, up for sale by auction to be held at the Sportsman Hotel, Castle Street, Caernarfon, but for whatever reason, it was not sold.

Things then went from bad to worse for the family, David Charles Pritchard was declared bankrupt and they returned to Caernarfon to live. According to his grandson, Richard Bonner Pritchard, his father, who was also called Richard Bonner Pritchard, often spoke to him of those days at the beginning of the 20th century. He and his two brothers, Charles and Bob, used to walk daily to the Sailing Club where they were given free meals, and his name for that unpleasant journey was the 'Walk of Shame'.

The three brothers, at an early age, decided upon a career at sea, as many other young Caernarfon lads did at that time. Charles and Richard joined the Merchant Navy during World War I, with the youngest brother Bob, following in their footsteps shortly after the end of the War, but all three returned to their home town early in the 1920s.

Charles was the first to return and he started up in business by hiring rowing boats in Porth yr Aur. In 1927, the year their father died, Richard was fortunate in securing a contract to transport materials to and from the Castle by the then Ministry of Works. On the strength of this he bought a lorry which formed the beginnings of a successful business called 'Pritchard

Brothers, Removals' in partnership with his younger brother, Bob. Charles also joined them and his duties were shared between boat hiring and other local work which included meeting the first train to arrive at Caernarfon station early every morning.

However, to return to the names of those who ran the Aber or Coed Helen Ferry, one will undoubtedly have realized by now that there were two persons named David Pritchard, who spent years transporting passengers across the mouth of the Seiont estuary, which prompts the question: 'Which one was the original Dafydd 'R Aber to the natives of the town?'. Was it the father, David Pritchard, (1808-84) or was it David Charles Pritchard, (1851-1927)? And to whom does the ditty, 'Mae cwch Dafydd 'R Aber ar y môr' (Dafydd 'R Aber's boat is on the sea) that has been sung by generations of Caernarfon children refer?

While researching for information about this

family, Mr Richard Bonner Pritchard gave me a copy of a painting of his great-grandfather and on the back of the painting the following words are inscribed: David Pritchard (1808-84).

This may hold the

answer to the question and that the ditty dates back to the third or even last quarter of the 19th century. Who knows?

There are usually four verses to the ditty and they can be translated thus:

1. Dafydd 'R Aber's boat is on the sea,
   Dafydd 'R Aber's boat is on the sea.
   O-oh! Dafydd 'R Aber's boat, Dafydd 'R Aber's boat,
   Dafydd 'R Aber's boat is on the sea.

2. It is full of red herrings, so they say, etc.

3. And they are truly stinking, so they say, etc.

4. They are good enough for the English, so they say, etc.

Sir Llewelyn Turner (1823–1903)

If there is one person that deserves to be hailed as the greatest benefactor of all time in the town of Caernarfon, then one should have no hesitation in naming Llewelyn Turner. He was a man of his time, but also a visionary and one worthy of being called a great man, as the poet states:

> Lives of great men all remind us we can make our lives sublime
> And departing leave behind us footprints on the sands of time.

We honour Llewelyn Turner for what he left behind. He was very much a man of his time having been born the eleventh child of William and Jane Turner of Parkia in 1823, 14 years before Queen Victoria ascended the throne; he was four years her junior and died two years after her death. He lived through the developments of the Victorian era and to give some idea of how Caernarfon's population increased during the early 19th century, the 1801 Census shows a figure of 3,626 which was twice the population of Bangor at 1,770. However, by the 1861 Census the population of Caernarfon had almost trebled to over 9,500.

With a name like Llewelyn one would expect that he was of old Welsh stock, but that was not so. Although his mother, Jane Williams was Welsh-born and even a descendant of Griffith Williams, Bishop of Ossary in Ireland, his father, William, was born in Lancashire, the sixth child in a large family who lived on a small estate called Low Mosshouse in Seathwaite. William's father died when he was only twelve years old and his godfather, a clergyman named the Rev. Robert Walker, became responsible for his education.

Under the guidance of the Rev. Walker, William took a keen interest in geology and also in a small slate quarry on the estate, and decided at an early age on a career in that industry. He received the sum of £500 from the family to set himself up as a partner in a quarry in Llanrwst. This first venture, although enabling him to earn a living, was not that profitable and he decided to form a company to work the Diffwys Quarry in Blaenau Ffestiniog and this turned out to be a lucrative venture. So much so indeed, that he was later approached by Mr Thomas Assheton Smith of the Vaynol Estate and made an offer to become a partner in the much larger Dinorwig Quarry. One condition laid down by the Squire was that he was to take up residence at Parkia, and that is how the family moved to Caernarfon.

The history of the success of the Dinorwig Quarry speaks for itself and it is no wonder that the Turner family prospered in the Caernarfon area. However, not all of William Turner's children were as interested in the slate quarrying industry as he was, and although his son of the same name earned a good living as a slate entrepreneur and owner of the Glynrhonwy Quarry in Llanberis, it was as a law attorney that his youngest son, Llewelyn Turner trained, becoming what we would call today a solicitor in 1847, aged 24.

That was the year that young Llewelyn, a keen yachtsman, (and to quote a rugby term, scored his first try). He was the owner of a very fast yacht and used to compete successfully at regattas both far and wide. He became friendly with a young London barrister, William Knight, who was a Rear Commodore of the Royal Harwich Yacht Club, and it was he who persuaded him to form a yacht club at Caernarfon. This he did and, with the aid of a letter from his friend to the Lord Commissioners of the Admiralty, was given permission for the new 'Welsh Yacht

Club' to fly the Blue Ensign. The Club also made a successful application for Royal Patronage to the Dowager Queen Adelaide, widow of King William IV, which resulted in it being renamed the 'Royal Welsh Yacht Club'. Royal Patrons since then have been King Edward VII, George V, George VI and the present Patron is HRH Prince Philip, Duke of Edinburgh. Llewelyn Turner served the Club as a flag officer for the remainder of his life. In his early days he was also active with the Lifeboat Society and took part in rescues resulting in the saving of lives. It can be said of him that it was as a solicitor that he earned a living, but he was a sailor at heart.

While still a comparatively young man, he took an interest in local government, becoming a member of the Town Council, following in the footsteps of his brother, Thomas Turner, a wine merchant and his brother-in-law, John Morgan, a banker and husband of his sister, Agnes, They both served as Mayors of Caernarfon, John Morgan in 1836-7 and again in 1852 and Thomas Turner from 1847 to 1849. Ten years later, and at the age of 36, Llewelyn Turner was elected Mayor and he became the longest serving Mayor since the passing of the Municipals Corporation Act of 1835. His term of office ran for a period of eleven years from 1859 to 1870 and during that time he was responsible for introducing improvements to the town in general.

As mentioned previously, there had been a dramatic increase in the population of the town during the first half of the 19th century, mainly due to the importance of Caernarfon as a slate exporting port and people from the rural areas had moved to this town in droves to find more lucrative work. This necessitated the building of what can only be described as jerry built houses in the centre of the town, with little regard for basic human requirements such as an adequate supply of clean water and a proper drainage system.

The Mayor realized that the implications of this could result in a serious health hazard as had been prophesied by an adverse report submitted by two local doctors in the mid 1840s. He made several attempts to persuade the Town Council to invest in a new reservoir to cater for all the town's needs, but on each occasion he failed to obtain a majority of the councillors to agree to this. The reason given was that they considered such a costly programme would mean a substantial increase in the rates and, that in reality, it was unlikely that such a catastrophe would ever come about.

In 1866, however, that which had been predicted by both the doctors and the Mayor did happen in the form of a visitation of the cholera. On 5 October, a two-year-old child from Crown Street, Caernarfon, died and the official cause of death was given as 'diarrhoea'. However, on 17 October, a four-year-old boy from nearby Turf Square, Simon, son of Joseph Hobley, druggist, died in similar circumstances, but on this occasion the dreaded word 'cholera' appeared on the death certificate. Then on 7 November, Mr Hugh Owen, Castle Square, treasurer of Engedi C. M. Chapel and a person of considerable influence in the town, succumbed to the pestilence. It was his death that made local doctors realise that they were witnessing what later proved to be the start of an epidemic.

By the end of November, 15 had died of the disease and another 52 in the following month, with as many as nine burials taking place on some days, five internments on 24 December. Even on Christmas Day itself, two people were buried, one of whom was Mr William Owen, Caernarfon's Harbour-master.

It was then, at the height of the epidemic, that a government medical officer was sent to Caernarfon on 23 December. His terms of reference were to assist the local board in its efforts to combat the disease and report on the situation.

Among the persons whom the Mayor had selected to act as members of the Local Health Board were two ministers of religion: the Vicar of the parish of Llanbeblig, the Rev. James Crawley Vincent and the Rev. Robert Ellis, (bardic name Cynddelw), minister of Caersalem Baptist Chapel. Both these gentlemen are reported to have carried out sterling work during the epidemic. The meetings were held under the chairmanship of the Mayor, Llewelyn Turner, at the Guild Hall daily at 9 a.m. prompt during those dark days and, according to reports, woe betide anyone who arrived late. At a time when some ministers left the area for fear of becoming victims of the disease, the Vicar and the Rev. Ellis remained loyal to their calling and stayed behind to administer to the sick and to the bereaved.

On arriving at Caernarfon, Dr Seaton, the Government Medical Officer was taken around the town by the Mayor and shown the areas where the epidemic had struck. Before leaving he left a copy of the report of his findings, which he would be presenting to his superiors. His report was a condemnation of the unsatisfactory state of cleanliness in the town in general and he dwelled on the deficiencies that had previously been pointed out to the Council by the Mayor. He further made a recommendation that no water should be drunk before first having been boiled and that notices to this effect should be placed in strategic points in the town.

It took a further 18 days and 15 more deaths from the date of Dr Seaton's arrival in Caernarfon for the town to be rid of the disease. As a result of his adverse report the Town Council was forced to take action and to do so in haste. From then on the Mayor held the whip hand and a government loan of £10,000 was negotiated to help finance a new water supply scheme for the town. The stranglehold that the majority of the Councillors had over the purse strings had finally been broken and, from then on, further improvements began to take place in the town. Within 15 months of the end of the epidemic, Caernarfon had its new water supply and its arrival was celebrated with the building of the fountain on Castle Square, which was officially opened on 25 April 1868, by the then Prince of Wales, later to become King Edward VII.

Hitherto, we have only discussed the achievements of Llewelyn Turner as Mayor and his deep interest in the sea and in sailing. However, we must not overlook the fact that he earned his living as a solicitor in the town for many years and, according to the Census of 1851, he was 28 years of age, unmarried and lived at no. 1 Church Street, where his office was situated. Two years later, he was appointed by the court in Caernarfon to defend a man accused of murder. His name was John Roberts, also known as Jack Swan after the name of the area where he lived in the Conwy Valley. He was arrested for mortally shooting a young teacher named Jesse Roberts in Ro-wen near Conwy. He insisted on pleading his innocence even though the strength of evidence against him seemed watertight and, at first, refused legal representation, but the magistrates appointed the young Llewelyn Turner to be responsible for his defence.

The solicitor visited his client to discuss the case and it soon became evident that the evidence against Jack was indeed damning, since one person had stated that he had offered to sell him a silver watch that belonged to the person who had been shot. When Jack heard this from the lips of his attorney, he then suggested that it may be better to have two solicitors quoting: 'two heads are better than one'. But, on reflection and under the circumstances a dozen of the best legal minds in the country could not have saved him from the gallows.

It was no surprise, therefore, that the Court found Jack Swan guilty of the offence and he was sentenced to death, but Jack was shocked by the verdict and on his return to the prison said to the Chief Warder: 'I did not expect this'. Later, however, he told him he believed that a petition on his behalf sent to the Queen could save his life.

Some days later the High Sheriff accompanied by Llewelyn Turner and the Chaplain visited him to explain the hopelessness of the situation. The following day Jack confessed to the Chaplain that it was he who had shot Jesse Roberts and that he fell dead without uttering a word. He also admitted to stealing the silver watch and that he had not bought it as he had stated in Court.

Jack Swan tried a further twice to cheat the course of justice. Firstly, he made accusations against a man named William Evans by stating that it was he who had persuaded him to shoot Jesse Roberts and that he loaned the gun and gave him 23 shillings to commit the crime. Apparently William Evans' son and Jesse Roberts were both applicants for a teaching post, and it was the latter who had been appointed. William Evans was arrested and taken to face his accuser at Caernarfon Jail, but it soon became evident that Jack Swan was lying and Evans was subsequently freed. The second time was on the last Saturday night that Jack spent on earth when he attempted to escape, but was soon captured.

After another talk with the Chaplain, Jack Swan admitted everything stating that William Evans had no part whatsoever in the murder of Jesse Roberts. He spent the remainder of his time in prayer, repenting for his sins, and on the morning of 10 August 1853 was executed. He was the first of three to face capital punishment within the walls of Caernarfon Jail. The last public execution took place on Morfa Seiont on Wednesday, 4 September 1822. It was there that Lewis Owen was hung for attempting to murder a Mr Sturdy, a supervisor from Conwy.

The case of Jack Swan was a one-off historical experience in defending a person facing a murder charge for Llewelyn Turner and one that was not to be repeated. He was connected with the law throughout his life and was highly thought of by judges and barristers on the circuit, many of whom were personal friends of his and had stayed at Parkia from time to time. He was a Justice of the Peace and Chairman of the Bench for many years and served as High Sheriff for Caernarfonshire in 1886-7.

He was a solicitor and of that there was no doubt, but he was no ordinary solicitor. Indeed there was nothing ordinary about Llewelyn Turner and for that we should be grateful. In whatever field he took an interest, one could be certain that improvements would soon appear in that field, because he had the talent of a true visionary. He was certainly the greatest visionary that 19th century Caernarfon ever produced and when was his like ever seen since?

The best example of Llewelyn Turner's prowess as a visionary has survived him, and is still here today for us to gaze and be amazed at, and that is Caernarfon Castle. Llewelyn Turner had from an early age taken a keen interest in Caernarfon Castle and had made it known that he saw a great potential in the edifice as a tourist attraction, but that much renovation work was required before attracting visitors from far and wide. He was said to be disappointed when the post of Deputy Constable become vacant and that he had not been considered due to his being regarded as too young. In fact, it was his brother-in-law, John Morgan, husband of his elder sister, Agnes, a successful banker and twice former Mayor of Caernarfon, who was appointed. During his term of office, John Morgan did commence on the renovation work and paid for a new gate at the main entrance known as the King's Gate in 1853. This large gate, made of oak, followed the same pattern as that of the entrance to Carlisle Castle.

It was in the year 1870, following the death of John Morgan and shortly after Llewelyn Turner's eleven-year term of office as Mayor, that the Constable of the Castle, Lord Caernarfon, wrote to him offering him the opportunity to become his deputy. Upon taking up the post, one of the first things that Llewelyn Turner did was to sack the mason who had been accountable to John Morgan for carrying out renovation work. The work that had been carried out under his supervision was regarded as shoddy and a new mason, called John Jones, was employed by the Deputy Constable and both men worked closely together for over 30 years to get the building up to the standard that it is today.

Much of the work that had been carried out by his predecessor had to be demolished and rebuilt by John Jones and his team of workmen. Some of the towers had to be reroofed and refloored. Nearly all the battlements had to be completely rebuilt and at least one tower restored. All of this work was costly, and even though Llewelyn Turner was successful in raising funds for some of the improvements, it is known for a fact that he had to dig deep into his own pocket to ensure that this important venture did not end up in debt.

At the same time, Llewelyn Turner insisted that the townspeople of Caernarfon should not have to pay an entrance fee to visit the Castle and that the way to help maintain this historic building was to charge visitors for the privilege. And now, more than a century after his death, the same ruling applies.

We, the people of Caernarfon today, take pride in the fact that our town is a World Heritage Centre. Thanks to whom? Thanks to two persons in particular. Firstly to a man born to a wealthy family, Llewelyn Turner, who recognized a potential in a ruin built by a conquering King in 1283, and secondly, to a Welsh craftsman, John Jones, who thoroughly deserved to be called John Jones, Castell Caernarfon (John Jones, Caernarfon Castle).

Sir William Henry Preece
(1834–1913)

Some time ago I was allowed to make a copy of a postcard belonging to Mrs Karen Owen, daughter of the late Mr Meirion Roberts. He and I were former pupils of the Boys' School, South Penrallt, during the years leading up to World War II. The photo is that of the funeral of Sir William Preece on its way through the village of Caeathro to the cemetery at Llanbeblig in November 1913.

William was the son of R. M. Preece, Bryn Helen, South Road, Caernarfon and he had his early education in a school nearby, known as Ysgol Jones Bach after the last headmaster, who retired in 1917. The first owner of the school was the Rev. J. Hews Bransby and it was opened in 1836. R. M. Preece was a banker and broker in partnership with another former mayor, John Morgan, brother-in-law to the well known Sir Llewelyn Turner, (1823–1903). R. M. Preece himself served as Mayor from 1843 to 1845.

When William was eleven years old he was sent to London for his education and it is not difficult to envisage the tiresome journey that faced him. The railway had yet to reach north Wales and one had to sail from Menai Bridge to Liverpool on a slow steamer called Erin-go-Bragh. Following an overnight's stay at the Adelphi Hotel, an eleven-hour journey to London ensued, including an hour's stay in Birmingham.

He was then educated at King's College, London, where he studied Science. Professor Cowper took him to see the Crystal Palace in Hyde Park that was built to house The Great Exhibition of 1851. As a science student William Preece attended the lectures of Michael Faraday and he once said that there was more romance in Faraday's lecture on 'The Candle' than in all the operas, dramas and books he had ever seen. Faraday was his hero and it became William's ambition to be Faraday's assistant. This was realized in 1853 when he was only 19 years old.

As a young man he also took a keen interest in sports and athletics and was cricket team captain of King's College School 11 in 1848-49. Later he became an enthusiastic yachtsman and also spent much of his leisure time practising shooting.

When William was 18 years of age he went to work in the offices of a civil servant named Edwin Clarke, who was responsible for the iron work under Robert Stevenson, the engineer who built the Britannia Bridge which was opened in 1850. During the following period, William Preece was a regular visitor to north Wales, as one who considered the bridge to be the eighth wonder of the world. Later he went to work for the Electric and International Telegraphic Company and the International Telegraphic Company, followed by the Channel Islands Telegraphic Company. from whence he was transferred to the Post Office in 1870 as a regional telegraphic engineer to start with, and then as chief telegraphic engineer. He served his last employer for 29 years before his retirement in 1899.

His main interest during these years was in the field of telegraphy and early in his life he was of the opinion that sound could be transmitted from one place to another without the use of wires. He lectured on this subject frequently and had the talent to make it sound interesting to the man in the street.

During his lifetime he carried out several experiments that were instrumental in bringing improvements to the lives of his contemporaries. He was the first to introduce electric bells to Britain from Paris, where he saw them for the first time. Then after personally experiencing the use of Alexander Graham Bell's telephones in the USA in 1877 he brought some back to Britain with him, and the following year had the honour of exhibiting how the system worked to Queen Victoria. He experimented with telegraphy before Marconi was born and sent a wireless message in 1882, when the Italian was only eight years old.

When Guglielmo Marconi came to Britain for the first time in 1896, Preece persuaded the Government to support him and thus establish a foundation for a large development in the field of wireless. It was he also who had Marconi establish the station at Waunfawr, not far from his home, Penrhos, Caeathro, where he went to live after retiring in 1899.

Though he spent over half a century in London, it was back to the Caernarfon area, his home town, that he came to reside in the autumn years of his life. He left Caernarfon aged eleven and soon afterwards his father and the whole family moved to London to live, but he always considered himself to be a native of the old town and the residents were pleased to welcome him back. As proof of that the Town Council honoured him. In 1899 he was made a Freeman of the Town of Caernarfon and at that time it was an unique honour in that he was the first ever recipient.

Later in the 20th century, in the year 1953, 40 years after Sir William Preece's death, the Rotary Club of Caernarfon had a commemorative plaque made for him and it is fitting that it should have been placed on the wall of the General Post Office in Castle Square.

Sir William Preece died at Penrhos on 6 November 1913, and was buried in Llanbeblig cemetery and seldom was such a funeral seen in the Caernarfon area. A large number of people came to pay their last respects to a man who was a pioneer in his field.

Air Ace and Distinguished Yachtsman Lionel Wilmot Brabazon Rees, VC, OBE, MC, AFC

Brabazon Rees was born in Plas Llanwnda, Castle Street, Caernarfon in 1884 and his family was well-known in the town. James Rees, his grandfather, a native of Carmarthen and an apprenticed printer, came to the town from London in 1831. William Potter & Company settled in Caernarfon with the intention of publishing a radical local newspaper and James Rees was made foreman. They published the *Caernarfon and Denbigh Herald*, which soon became a popular weekly newspaper.

In 1840 William Potter decided to retire and James Rees became the new owner of the newspaper. In 1855 a sister paper in Welsh, *Yr Herald Cymraeg* was published and James Evans, Cae Llenor, became its editor. James Rees retired in 1871 and James Evans followed him as proprietor. Unfortunately, two of James Rees' sons who were involved in the business had died and no other member of the family wished to take over.

James Rees's son, Colonel Charles H. Rees, a Caernarfon solicitor was the father of Lionel and his younger sister, Muriel. It is said that they were both very close and that Muriel idolized her brother. They had a very happy childhood and it is recorded that Lionel's favourite pastime was flying his kite on the quay nearby and according to the testimony of his contemporaries, he was the champion amongst them and they were amazed at his mastery of the skill. Could it be a sign of things to come?

Young Lionel followed his father into the army and was educated at Eastbourne College and the Military Academy, Woolwich. He joined the Royal Garrison Artillery in 1903 and spent years in the Middle East, where he became interested in geology and divinity and in 1914 was transferred as a lieutenant into the Royal Flying Corps, where he served and fought in World War I.

He trained as a pilot and soon mastered the skills

of flying and of combat in the air. He became one of the most successful airmen for shooting down enemy planes and was promoted from rank to rank, ending the war as a group captain and regarded as the highest decorated air ace of World War I. These decorations included the Victoria Cross, Military Cross and Air Force Cross.

In the Honours List in 1919 he was awarded an OBE and in 1920 the Caernarfon Borough Council extended the Freedom of the Borough to him and he was presented with an expensive ceremonial sword.

One would expect that he would have had more than his share of honours by then, but that was not so. He was a member of the Royal Welsh Yacht Club, Caernarfon, in Porth yr Aur and the owner of a twelve ton Loch Fyne yacht named *May*, built in Scotland in 1902 and powered by a two-cylinder Kelvin paraffin engine.

In 1933 Brabazon Rees decided to face a new challenge by attempting to cross the Atlantic single-handed in the *May*, starting the voyage from Porth yr Aur on 2 July. It is good to be able to quote an eye witness' account of that historical afternoon. Richard Trefor Jones, (Dic), a native of Caernarfon, who in the 1950s emigrated to Canada, was on the quay. He was 22 years old at the time and watched Brabazon Rees on the slipway preparing the *May* for the voyage and waiting for the tide, so that he could tend to the ropes and thus allow the stern to enter the stream coming from the river Seiont, under the Aber Bridge and into the Menai Strait in front of the Yacht Club. The Mayor and Councillors were there to wish the Group Captain well and after shaking hands he untied the ropes and commenced on his adventurous and dangerous voyage. Dic stayed in Porth yr Aur watching the *May* approaching the entrance to Caernarfon bar and gradually disappearing from sight.

The voyage came to a successful end on 21 October 1933. The *May* arrived at Nassau in the Bahamas after two months and 20 days at sea and this achievement brought Brabazon Rees to the notice of the wide world outside his own country and home town. When the Cruising Club of America came to learn of this, they set about honouring him with the Blue Water Medal. This is a very special honour as only one medal per annum is presented by the club.

Compared with Dic Trefor, who crossed the Atlantic over 50 times to visit his home town, Brabazon Rees did not return to Caernarfon after leaving in 1933. He settled in the Bahamas, married a local girl and died there on 28 September 1955. He did, however, present his Blue Water Medal to his old yacht club in Porth yr Aur and there it remains eshibited, a rare and valuable treasure in the club's possession.

It should be noted, however, that Brabazon Rees

The Cruising Club of America's 'Blue Water Medal'

did return to Britain twice. The first time was during World War II to rejoin the RAF at the beginning of 1942, but he could only stay for four days before being posted to the Middle East to command an aerodrome there.

Two years later and due to ill health, he was discharged and returned to the Bahamas. Then in 1953, suffering from leukaemia, he was admitted to RAF Hospital Uxbridge for treatment. He would have liked to visit his home town on that occasion, but his health would not allow it so he sent a letter to the Mayor of Caernarfon apologizing:

When I was faced with difficulties, I would say

to myself what would a Freeman of the Town of Caernarfon do in this situation? Invariably the answer would come to me. He would carry on without delay. That I would do, and the difficulties would disappear.

A Musical Family

Have you ever thought what Caernarfon was like during the latter 19th and early 20th century? It was a hard life for the majority with much poverty, yet many people succeeded in business and slates from the nearby quarries provided work for those loading vessels in the harbour. Others earned their living as seafarers and there were several shipbuilders and foundries in the town, employing craftsmen, skilled engineers and apprentices.

Many ships from other countries visited the town and, as one would expect, the public houses were kept busy. Caernarfon was called 'Tref y Trigain Tafarn' (Town of the three score taverns). Here also were houses of ill repute where the pleasures of the flesh were available on demand. But there was another side to Caernarfon, religion and culture also prospered here. Another name for the town was 'Prifddinas yr Inc' (Capital of the ink) referring to the printing industry, for there were many printers and publishers who produced newspapers, religious journals, educational books and so forth.

Society, therefore, was a mixture of the good and the bad and similar to that found in any port in the country. The good, however, was represented by the

Welsh puritan tradition, and it is the history of one such family that is the subject of this chapter – the Williams family. Four generations of musicians who lived here in the town of Caernarfon.

One of them, John Williams a blacksmith, and a member of the Wesleyan chapel, made a name for himself as a composer of hymn tunes. It is said that one of his compositions was very popular amongst members of that denomination and he named it Pool Street, after the street where he lived. Unfortunately, however, and despite several attempts by the present writer to obtain a copy of this hymn tune, the quest has proved unsuccessful and the tune does not appear in any modern hymn book.

John Williams' son, Humphrey Williams, watchmaker, 6 Pool Street, was also a talented musician and conductor of a well-known choir in its day, The Welsh Harmonics, referred to in the late Dr Gwilym Arthur Jones' book *Pobol Caernarfon ac Addolwyr Engedi* (1992).

Humphrey Williams had three sons, John, Robert and Howel, who entertained many audiences far and wide with their musical talents when they were young. Ann, the wife of Humphrey Williams, died at the age of 44 on 2 December 1866 and she was buried the following day in Llanbeblig cemetery. This was at a time when nearly 100 Caernarfon people died of the cholera epidemic of 1866–1867, but proof was not found that she died of the pestilence, although nine people were buried in the cemetery on the same day, and most of them were certified as having died of cholera.

The children were aged between six and ten when their mother died and their father deserved all praise for bringing them up and for the accolade that they achieved as soloists, instrumentalists and conductors at an early age.

It was Robert who starred as a soloist, Howel as an exceptionally good violinist, and John stood in front of audiences regularly as a soloist, instrumentalist and conductor.

Howel was taught to play the violin in Liverpool and at the Caernarfon National Eisteddfod of 1877, the first to be held at the Pavilion, he had the honour of being leader of the orchestra at the age of 16. He was presented with a gold medal for his performance and was photographed in the company of the Eisteddfod's adjudicators and artists. He also had a fine voice and at an early age sang alto in local choirs and later became a choir conductor in the footsteps of his father and brother John.

He could well have become a musician of repute, but like many other young men of Caernarfon he was attracted to a life at sea. He sailed as an apprentice on the *Bell of Arvon* (Captain Jones), but on arriving in San Francisco he left the ship. It is not known what his intentions were at the time – to look for work, perhaps, and settle in the USA. This is a mystery, but the fact is that he stayed there for two or three years until a mate called Richard Jones on the ship *King Cedric* (Captain D. Elias of Caernarfon) came across him in San Francisco and persuaded the captain to take him on as a member of the crew on the homeward voyage.

One night, when the ship was awaiting loading in Queenstown, Richard Jones began to sing to the accompaniment of Howel on the violin and they received a deafening ovation from sailors and yachtsmen anchored nearby.

After returning home to Caernarfon, Howel again went to sea and decided to study in earnest for his examinations to qualify for his master's ticket. Eventually he succeeded and was employed as a mate on an Elder Dempster Company ship the *Merrimac*. Then, on 2 April 1895, fortune smiled on him. A ship was observed in difficulty and Captain Morgan of the *Merrimac* sent Howel across to her in a boat. He returned and reported to the captain that there was no-one on the ship and that the cargo had moved causing the ship to list badly. The captain agreed for Howel and a ship's carpenter to reboard the ship to carry out further inspection. This was done and they convinced the captain that they were of the opinion that the cargo could be trimmed. The following morning nine sailors were sent to assist Howel with the job of righting the cargo. During the day, the *Merrimac* attempted to tow the ship, but the rope broke. The captain sent another four sailors to the ship and with their help, working through the night, the ship was righted.

Ten of the sailors volunteered to sail the ship back to Britain under the command of Howel and in his own words he describes what happened afterwards:

We succeeded in bending the sails and sailed for the Channel. We got around Cape Clear on 22 April, not having seen land until then. We hove to in a severe gale on the 23, having picked up a safe anchorage. We dropped anchor in Cardigan Bay, and wired Liverpool for a tug. That evening Captain Rattery the Co. Marine Superintendent and seven men arrived in a tug and took us in tow and anchored her in the Mersey on 25 April. Later she was taken to the Herculaneum Dock, Liverpool. She had been navigated 1,700 miles. Thus the vessel that had been abandoned was restored with her cargo to the owners.

For this brave act Howel was promoted captain on one of the Elder Dempster ships. The *S.S. Loango* and on his first voyage as master, Captain Howel Williams went to help another ship that had lost a propeller and towed it to Madeira. He did not, however, enjoy a long period as a ship's master due to his eyesight deteriorating and he was forced to retire early.

He died on 6 June 1926, aged 65 and lies buried in Llanbeblig with his wife, Margaret Elizabeth, who died on 17 November 1901, aged 38. They had three children, two sons and a daughter. His second son, John Richardson Williams, drowned, having been swept overboard from the ship *S.S. New Brighton* two days off Cape Verde Islands on 18 February 1925, aged 29.

It is not possible to know what successes Howel Williams would have achieved had he decided on a career in music, but it would appear that the sea was his first love, even taking into consideration those early days in San Francisco.

Hitherto, we have only discussed members of the family who were musicians who earned a living by other means: John Williams, the composer of hymn tunes who was a blacksmith by trade; his son Humphrey, a watchmaker, who was also a choirmaster; and his son Howel, the instrumentalist who became a sea captain. However, Howel's eldest brother, John, became a professional musician, even though the 1881 Census describes him as a watchmaker like his father, aged 24, and that the family had moved from 6 Pool Street to 20 Castle Square, which was only across the road in fact. But by 1895, according to *Slaters Directory*, he is referred to as a teacher of music, living at Preswylfa. By this time, he was also a paid organist at Christ Church, Caernarfon. His father Humphrey died in

1883 and by 1895, again according to *Slaters*, Williams & Pritchard, Watchmakers & Music Warehouse were the occupants of 20 Castle Square. It is likely that John had gone into partnership and extended the business to include musical instruments.

He was born in the year 1856 and it is known that his career as choirmaster began in 1875 when he was only 19 years old and the following year, 1876, his choir won in the National Eisteddfod at Wrexham. His record in the National Eisteddfod is one to be coveted. He won six first prizes and one second prize in competitions for mixed and male voice choirs. Côr Meibion Eryri beat three other choirs from all over Wales in the London Welsh Eisteddfod in 1897 held at the Queen's Hall. After the competition, Mr David Lloyd George MP took the members on a tour around the Houses of Parliament and the following day the choir sang at the Surveyor's Institute, Westminster. The president of that meeting was no less a person

John Williams and his choir

than Caernarfon born Sir William Preece to whom there is a plaque on the post office in Castle Square, Caernarfon.

Probably John Williams' two greatest achievements as choirmaster were at the London National Eisteddfod in 1909 and the National Eisteddfod in Wrexham, 1912, when his choir beat all the best choirs in south Wales and through these successes Cymdeithas Gorawl Caernarfon became the undisputed best choir in Wales. In a tribute to him in the *Caernarfon and Denbigh Herald* dated 30 November 1917, following his untimely death, it was stated that John Williams was one of the two best choirmasters in Britain. Not only Wales, but Britain, and what accounted for his success as an instructor was the talent he had for analysing a piece of music and teaching the members of the choir to sing it exactly in the way the composer had intended for it to be sung. He paid particular attention to the words and made the music subordinate to the words rather than vice versa. He took the trouble of explaining the meaning of the words in detail, how to pronounce them and where to stress certain syllables or words. He believed wholeheartedly that the music should be the accompaniment for the words.

In 1899, Côr Meibion Eryri sang in Caernarfon Castle in front of the Duke and Duchess of York, later to become King George V and Queen Mary, and at the end of that year the choir was invited to sing at Windsor Castle, by royal command, and amongst the audience were the Prince and Princess of Wales and the Emperor and Empress of Germany. Queen Victoria was unable to attend due to a bereavement in the family. The members of the Royal Family were greatly pleased with the performance and at the end of the concert the Prince of Wales – on behalf of the Queen – presented John Williams with an expensive diamond-studded baton as a token of appreciation. The choir also had a new name Côr Meibion Brenhinol Eryri (The Royal Eryri Male Voice Choir) and from then on they were in great demand and sang in many towns and cities in England such as Northampton, Kettering and Wolverhampton, but by the end of the year the choir had dispersed.

In the meantime the Caernarfon Operatic Society, under the guidance of John Williams, was formed. Many of the Gilbert and Sullivan favourites *HMS Pinafore*, *Mikado* and *Pirates of Penzance* were staged and the proceeds went towards the cost of building the Cottage Hospital, which was opened in 1900. John Williams, himself, took on the main male parts in the performances, but after a few years he decided against continuing as director and that signalled the end of the Operatic Society. He re-established the Choral Society and in 1911, he conducted the choir at the Investiture of the Prince of Wales at Caernarfon Castle. The choir's performance on that day was such a success that innumerable requests for its services followed and concerts were held in London, Liverpool and other large cities in the United Kingdom. Afterwards, there was no doubt that John Williams of the Caernarfon Choral Society was the most popular choirmaster in the whole of Britain. But he was still Joni Williams, Côr Mawr to the good people of Caernarfon, and I recall listening to my mother and aunts reminiscing about the time they spent in their youth as members of his choir.

There can be no doubt that he was the most noted member of this exceptionally talented musical family, three generations of which have been noted and one remains. John Williams had five children, two sons and three daughters. The eldest was William Humphrey Williams, born in 1891, and the second son was the youngest child, John, who was ten years younger than his brother.

At the age of twelve William Humphrey trained as a chorister in Magdalen College, Oxford, where he remained for four years and as he was one of the most promising there, he was often chosen to take part as a soloist. Then, under a scheme called ex-choristership, he spent a further twelve months at the college. Upon leaving, he commenced on a career in business with the Alexandra Slate Quarry in Caernarfon and two years later was apprenticed to Turner Brothers Asbestos and Rubber Manufacturers, Rochdale.

Soon after he completed his apprenticeship, war broke out and he was amongst the first to enlist in August 1914 as a second lieutenant in the Sixth Lancashire Fusiliers. In July 1915, after a period under instruction in Southport and Crowbridge, he was posted to the Dardanelles and he took part in the Gallipoli Campaign. In fact, he was the only officer in his company to survive. He could not, however, continue in that theatre of war as he was suffering from a poisoned arm. Then in November 1916, when he had recovered, he came home on leave to Caernarfon. By this time he had been promoted to lieutenant and was then posted to Alexandria in Egypt, where he joined the Royal Flying Corps and after three months training he passed as a pilot. He was again promoted to the rank of captain and within six months was made a flight commander. Then, on 3 March 1918, he joined a squadron in Palestine and on 3 May was killed in action in aerial combat with the enemy, exactly a fortnight after becoming engaged to marry a Miss Ormerod of Castleton, near Manchester. This was another severe blow to the family, as it was less than six months since the death of his father. His name and address W. H. Williams, Preswylfa, can be seen on the Cenotaph on Caernarfon's Castle Square.

His younger brother, John, also was at Magdalen College as a chorister for a period, but little is known about him. Only one fact was uncovered during my research, that Master John Williams was present at his father's funeral in November 1917.

The Show of the Century

Buffalo Bill (William Frederick Cody)

Exactly 110 years exactly ago to this year, on the 4 May 1904, something of importance occurred in Caernarfon and surprisingly enough it had nothing to do with the Religious Revival of that year in Wales. A large contingent of the Wild West came to town and the man responsible for this unique visit was no other than William Frederick Cody, commonly referred to as Buffalo Bill. He commenced his journey through north-west Wales with 800 performers from various countries together with 500 horses. He gave performances at Llandudno (2 May), Holyhead (3 May), Caernarfon (4 May), Porthmadog (5 May), before moving on to Dolgellau and from there to Aberystwyth.

W. F. Cody was born on 26 February 1846 near Le Claire, Iowa, and was one of the most colourful characters of the Wild West. He was a soldier in the American Civil War from 1863 to 1865. Then from 1868 to 1872 he served as chief scout for the Third Cavalry during the Plains Wars. He was promoted colonel and received the Medal of Honour in 1872. He had many other jobs including that of a hunter of bison and was contracted to the Kansas Pacific Railroad to supply their workmen with fresh meat. In a period of eight months it was said that he killed 4,860 of these animals and was given the name Buffalo Bill.

However, he was not the first to be known by that name. The first was a man called Comstock. Cody won the right to use the name following a contest with Comstock to see who could kill the most bison in a stipulated time. Cody was declared the winner.

In December 1872, Cody went to Chicago with a friend from Texas called Jack Omohundro, to commence on a new career as a performer in a show called *The Scouts of the Prairie*, one of the original Wild

West shows produced by Ned Buntline. During 1873–4 both men invited a friend to join them in a new drama, *Scouts of the Plains*. His name was James Butler Hickok, or 'Wild Bill Hickok' as he was known. This was to be the focus of his life from then on and he became extremely successful as a businessman, running his own business and going from strength to strength, until 1887 when he was invited to come to Britain to take part in Queen Victoria's Golden Jubilee Celebrations. He put on shows in London and Birmingham before moving on to Salford, near Manchester, where he performed regularly for five months.

In 1889 he went on tour through Europe and the following year he met Pope Leo XIII. Then in 1893 he exhibited during the renowned World Fair at Chicago and became extremely popular and even world-famous.

But, let us return to the year 1904 and his visit to the counties of Caernarfonshire and Anglesey, and especially so to the town of Caernarfon. It is understood that the town's schools were closed for the day, so as to give the children an opportunity to visit this unique exhibition that portrayed the exciting history of part of the world that was familiar to all children. Performances were held twice daily, one at 2 p.m. in the afternoon and another at 8 p.m. in a large field on the Bethel Road.

Some of the main attractions seen by those who were present are recorded. The show was presented from a train, which included 60 carriages and arrived at Caernarfon Railway Station, drawn by six steam engines. It was a red letter day for those who paid an entrance fee of between one shilling and seven shillings and six pence to be able to boast 'I was there'.

At precisely 2 p.m. the Cowboy Band struck up the stirring notes of the 'Star Spangled Banner' which was a cue for the various Red Indian tribes, led by their chiefs to gallop forward in full war-paint and dress. The last of these chieftains was no less a person than the son and heir of the arch enemy of the Wild West pioneers, 'Sitting Bull' aptly called 'Young Sitting Bull' who received a warm reception.

The audience was entertained by several exhibitions of horse-riding by natives of such countries as Mexico, the Caucusus and America. There were also 16 members of the English Lancers who had seen action in the Boer War, as well as soldiers from the American Cavalry and other performers far too numerous to mention.

The main attraction, however, was a scene from Custer's Last Stand or the Battle of the Little Big Horn. That was a bloody battle fought between hundreds, if not thousands of American Indians under the leadership of 'Sitting Bull' and a small contingent of soldiers under the command of General Custer. It was revealed that the chief scout, Buffalo Bill, did not arrive at the scene until the following day, and was an eyewitness to the aftermath of that unforgettable massacre. He took the part of Custer in the scene.

It was the show of the century and no-one can deny that it was indeed an unique one. Caernarfon had not seen its like before or ever likely to see afterwards. W. F. Cody lived until the year 1917 and even though it was said that he lost much of the wealth he had earned during his career as a successful businessman, he left over $100,000 in his will. On his death on 10 January 1917, within six weeks of his 71st birthday, tributes were received from King George V of Britain, Kaiser Wilhelm II of Germany and President Woodrow Wilson of the United States. He was buried in Elks Lodge Hall, Denver, and his friend Governor John B. Kendrick, Wyoming, led the funeral procession.

Some Feat over
a Century and a Half Ago

One wonders how many readers can believe that a man, in the year 1857, crossed from Caernarfon to Anglesey, without the aid of a boat and without having to swim across the Menai Strait. That was 157 years ago and I can well hear many saying: 'Well, he certainly did not fly across, because that was 52 years before Louis Blériot crossed the English Channel in an aeroplane from a village near Calais in France to Dover in England'. True enough, but it was possible to fly even in those days, not in an aeroplane perhaps, but in a balloon. On 19 September 1783, Pilatre de Rozier, a scientist, was the first to launch a hot air balloon named *Aerostat Reveillion* and his passengers were a sheep, a duck and a cockerel. The balloon remained in the air for 15 minutes before falling to the ground. Two months later on 21 November, Rozier and a friend were the first men to achieve a successful flight in a balloon and land safely.

In those days, Regatta Week at Caernarfon was one of the most important events of the year and people flocked to the quay to witness yachts racing on the Menai Strait, even railway companies reduced fares on the days when the annual regatta was held.

There were stalls on the quay and entertainment was provided for spectators, such as 'walking the greasy pole' where innumerable competitors ended up in the brine. Then on the last night of the regatta, according to custom, the organizers would hold a grand concert at the Castle. As part of the celebration in 1857, Mr Albion, the chief organizer, invited a Mr Goddard, the owner of a balloon, to come to the Castle and to ascend from there in his balloon and cross over to Anglesey.

One thing that should be remembered is that it would not have been possible to achieve this feat in any town or village, only in a place where a substantial supply of gas was at hand. There had been a gasworks in Caernarfon since the year 1832, the first town in Wales to receive this precious form of energy. The

The Regatta, 1908

The balloon above the Castle, 1857

city of Bangor followed in 1843 and in the first half of the 19th century they were the only two places with a gasworks until 1875 when one was built at Llandudno, followed by many more by 1880. The benefit which favoured Caernarfon and Bangor during those years was that they were ports and were able to import large amounts of coal. Therefore Mr Goddard could only have obtained the 20,000 cubic feet of gas required for his flight across the Strait in 1857 in Caernarfon or Bangor. The gas was transported to the Castle in a four-inch diameter pipe and by 6.30 p.m. that evening all was ready for this adventurous journey.

Then, with everyone watching expectantly, Mr Goddard entered the *Aurora,* as the balloon was called, and untied the ropes. Eventually, and to the deafening cheers of the crowd and melodious notes of the band, the balloon arose and went straight up. It was an interesting and exciting experience, the like of which had never been seen or would be repeated in the town.

The *Aurora* gained speed and went out of view in the clouds. Within an hour Mr Goddard allowed her to lose height gradually in order to be able to see his whereabouts and he soon realized that the balloon was about to come down near a large green buoy in the middle of the Strait. He had to change plan in haste and allow it to drift slowly in the direction of Anglesey. It appeared to take ages, but eventually the *Aurora* landed safely in Llanidan Park. Some local people came to his assistance to pack the balloon tidily and carry it to the ferry to be transported back to Caernarfon. This must have made them feel part of a historic occurrence of importance and an unforgettable experience.

In Llanidan, not only did Mr Goddard receive a welcome fit for a prince from the locals, but a Mr Parry entertained him and attended to all his needs upon his arrival. Later that evening the balloonist returned to Caernarfon and was seen sitting comfortably and smoking a cigar with friends around midnight.

The launching of the balloon was followed by a firework display and songs, both sad and humorous, were sung and the inside of the old Castle was effectively illuminated with many commenting that it was spectacular and second to none. The fête, under the supervision of Mr Albion, was highly praised in the press and deservedly so, as it had been so successful.

That was the end of a historical day in the month of

August 1857, in the age of the horse and cart, when a marvel without parallel was witnessed at Caernarfon. It cannot be difficult to imagine what the topic of conversation would have been among the slate loaders on the quay in the following days.

Entertainment in Days Gone By

In the preceding chapter, the reader had a glance at the type of entertainment that appealed to our forebears over a century ago. However, the Buffalo Bill Show of the century was a one-off never to be repeated event and one may well ask what our ancestors had to look forward to in the field of entertainment apart from that.

It must be remembered that 1904 was the year of the Religious Revival of 04-05, as it was called. The chapels and churches used to hold regular literary and musical competitions called Penny Readings. In 1877, however, due to the foresight of men such as Sir Llewelyn Turner, the large Caernarfon Pavilion holding 8,000 people was built, primarily to house the National Eisteddfod that year, and all types of entertaining activities were to take place there.

By the end of the first decade of the 20th century, however, cinemas were opened in all parts of the United Kingdom including one in Caernarfon in 1910 at the Guild Hall, Eastgate Street. The site was owned by the town council, and the cinema run by a married couple, Evan O. and Rose H. Davies, he a native of Conwy and she of Glyn Ceiriog. They came to Caernarfon from Holyhead where they owned two other cinemas, the New Town Cinema and the Empire.

The first films were shown in Caernarfon's Pavilion by a company called Cinematography, but on 1 August 1910, and only occasionally afterwards they were shown in the Guild Hall. However, in 1913, E. O. Davies obtained a licence for the hall to be a cinema on permanent lease by the town council. Of course, these were silent films and during the performances a pianist and sometimes a violinist would play their instruments. At first, it was Mr I.

The Guild Hall

Roberts who was the pianist, and it is said that he walked all the way from Llanwnda to his work. Many cinemagoers would call at Robinson's shop at the corner of Stryd Star Bach to buy liquorish to enjoy while watching the film.

It is difficult to know which film was the first to be shown in the Guild Hall, but in September 1910 the advertised film was called *Blue Bird*. Then in 1927, the first 'talkie' film was shown, *The Jazz Singer* starring Al Jolson (1886-1950). In 1930 E. O. Davies died and his wife, Mrs R. H. Davies, became responsible for the business for the next 20 years. They gave pleasure during the dark days of two world wars and for a further 15 years. E. O. Davies' death was recorded in the local paper as follows: 'A wreath by the town's people in kind remembrance of one who gave pleasure to the kiddies. The family were members of Ebenezer Wesleyan Chapel and he leaves a wife and two daughters Dilys and Eluned Lloyd Davies.'

Few people today can remember E. O. Davies as he died over 80 years ago, but many of us remember Mrs R. H. Davies and, on a personal note, I have a child's recollection of a third cinema being built in the town, the Majestic, in 1934. Before this time there were only two cinemas and as the Empire was specially built in 1915 by a man named Caradog Rowlands, both the Empire and Guild Hall

The 1950s Majestic staff

competed for business for almost 20 years before the opening of a new luxurious cinema to hold 1,050 people. I recall my aunt accompanying me to the garden of her house in Bangor Street to show me the partly built building and saying: 'That will be a new picturehouse and you will enjoy watching films there'. That was a true prophecy and I spent many hours at all three cinemas; The Guild Hall, The Empire and The Majestic. I also remember how popular the three cinemas were in the years of my youth and can still visualise the queues waiting outside in all weathers, before being allowed to enter into the warmth and out of the rain. Oh, how things have changed.

To return to the Guild Hall and its owner, Mrs R.

H. Davies, we, the children of the 1930s and early 1940s had to pay three pence to go to the Empire and Majestic on Saturday afternoons, but the Guild Hall only charged two pence, which meant we had a penny spare to spend on whatever we fancied. With many of us by then in our early teenage years, what we would do was to go to a shop in Bangor Street, run by an old lady called Mrs Williams, Ship and Castle. Outside the shop there were cigarette vending machines and for a penny we could have three SOS cigarettes, and after making sure we had enough matches, we would enjoy a smoke in the cinema's gallery, while watching *Flash Gordon* and a cowboy film to follow. At times we would get overexcited and start stamping the floor when the posse was on the point of catching up with the outlaws. It was then that the film would be stopped and Mrs Davies would appear on stage demanding silence with the aid of a broom handle striking the wooden stage floor. She would then give us a telling off stating that she would not continue the film and that we would be sent home without seeing it's end. It worked every time!

Mrs Davies died in 1951 and another company took over the cinema until 1960 when the cinema had to close due to the building becoming unsafe and the town council was not prepared to invest money due to the prohibitive cost.

The last film to be shown there, from Thursday to Saturday night, 21-23 July 1960, was *The Barbarians* starring Pierre Cressoy.

The Pavilion, Caernarfon

The Pavilion's Foundation Stone

At the beginning of the last quarter of the 19th Century a company was formed in Caernarfon to raise £7,000 capital to build the Pavilion, and the Mayor, Councillor Hugh Pugh and many other influential townsmen were behind the venture. The foundation stone was laid in Cae Twtil on 26 May 1877 and the building was completed within three months. The first public meeting held there was the opening ceremony of the 1877 National Eisteddfod on 21 August, six other National Eisteddfodau were also held there in 1880, 1886, 1894, 1906, 1921 and

1935, and it was considered to be an ideal venue for the nation's main festival.

Whilst the majority of the people in the area welcomed this 200 by 100 foot building, the Dinorwig Quarrymen were annoyed that Dixons of Liverpool had been given the contract to fit a corrugated iron roof on the building. Their choice, naturally, would have been a roof made of slate, and they went as far as to hold a protest march through the town and threatened never to set foot in the new building. But, after realizing the potential it had for shows, concerts and meetings of a religious and political nature, they relented and put an end to the boycott.

In 1878 the famous aerialist, Blondin, who had walked on a tightrope above Niagra Falls, appeared at the Pavilion and astonished his audience with a similar performance 40 feet above their heads.

Well-known names such as Bostock, Wilding and Teago and companies specializing in top-class entertainment came to the Pavilion and people from all over north Wales attended their performances. This was the largest building of its kind in Wales with a seating capacity for 8,000 and other towns were envious of Caernarfon.

Meetings of a religious nature with some of the best-known preachers of their day could attract a full house. During the 1904 Revival, no less a person

Building the Pavilion

Caernarfon's old Pavilion

than the Evan Roberts, the noted revivalist came to the Pavilion and after lesser-known preachers had addressed the congregation, he was asked to give testimony, but the great man refused on the grounds that he had not 'been moved by the Spirit'. The Rev. Jubilee Young preached a well known sermon by Christmas Evans and held the congregation spellbound. And it was not only Welsh-language preachers who graced the Pavilion stage, the evangelist Gipsy Smith came to the Pavilion twice, the first time in 1907 and again in 1931.

It should also be noted that large political meetings were held here in the Pavilion. Some of the better-known politicians of their day, members of all political parties, amongst them being: David Lloyd George, Winston Churchill, Austen Chamberlain, A. Bonar Law, Ernest Bevin and D. R. Greenfell, all representatives of the three parties that were in government in Westminster during the 20th century.

In 1904, Lloyd George and Winston Churchill were members of the Liberal Party and on 21 October both addressed a large audience from the Pavilion platform and received the warmest of welcomes. At the end of the meeting, they were both carried shoulder high all the way to Plas y Bryn, Bontnewydd, where they were staying. It was at that meeting that Lloyd George spoke of his vision for devolution for

England, Ireland, Scotland and Wales. His theme was 'Home Rule all round'.

Those are some of the highlights in the field of entertainment, religion and politics that took place at the Pavilion in its heyday. During World War I (1914-18), the Pavilion was a venue that continued to attract and provide high standards of entertainment for the people of the Caernarfon area, and in 1921 the National Eisteddfod of Wales was held there for the sixth time since the year it was built in 1877.

At that Eisteddfod both main competitions in the poetry section were won by Caernarfonshire poets, Mr R. J. Rowlands (Meuryn) born in Abergwyngregyn, near Bangor, winning the chair, and Pwllheli-born Rev. Albert Evans Jones (Cynan) being awarded the crown. Meuryn, a journalist by profession, composed an ode in strict metre 'Min y Môr' (By the Sea) where he was able to display his expertise to the full. Cynan on the other hand, in his poem 'Mab y Bwthyn' (Son of the Cottage), drew heavily on his wartime experiences both as a non-combatant stretcher-bearer and later as a chaplain. Both poems were extremely popular in their day and were to become test pieces in reciting and penillion singing competitions in subsequent Eisteddfodau for many years.

When cinemas became popular in the 1930s, and with three of them in Caernarfon, less and less use was made of the Pavilion. Nevertheless, concerts and dramas were performed there, and in one concert, Paul Robeson, the Negro spiritual singer took the stage there in September 1934, at the time of the Gresford Pit Disaster, near Wrexham, when 264 miners were killed in an explosion. Paul Robeson happened to be filming in the south Wales valleys at the time and had a high regard for the people of the mining communities whom he had met. He was deeply moved by the tragedy and gave a donation of £100 towards the fund that was established to assist the widows and orphans of those who had died.

After the concert there were another three meetings of importance held at the pavilion up to World War II: the Caernarfon National Eisteddfod in 1935; one to welcome the three Welsh Nationalists Saunders Lewis, The Rev. Lewis Valentine and D. J. Williams, upon their release from Wormwood Scrubs Prison in 1937, having been sentenced for an act of protest on behalf of their fellow-Welshmen and in the name of peace, by setting fire to a building at RAF Penrhos, Pwllheli; and thirdly the Labour Day Festival of 1938, which was addressed by D. R. Greenfell MP, in the absence of Clement Atlee. On the three occasions the building was filled to capacity. At the beginning of World War II in 1939, the Pavilion was requisitioned by the government and used as a warehouse, mainly to store food. There also, as I can well remember, we as a family were required to go to be fitted with our gas masks, and from then on we had to carry the gas masks everywhere, including to school – books in a satchel over one shoulder and the gas mask on a piece of string over the other.

The Pavilion was on lease to the government until 1956. By this time the building had deteriorated considerably and much maintenance work was required on it. The borough council felt that it would be impracticable and too costly to repair the Pavilion, and that there was no longer a need for a building of this size, subsequently in 1961 it was decided that the building be demolished, despite the arguments of those who opposed the decision. It was on 21 October 1961 that the people of Caernarfon bade farewell to the Pavilion in real Welsh style.

The last farewell to the Pavilion had been arranged by the north Wales representative of the BBC, Mr Sam Jones. This was in two parts, firstly in the form of a hymn singing festival conducted by Madam Dilys Wynne Williams with Mr G. Peleg Williams as the accompanist, and secondly in the form of a radio pageant, again arranged by Mr Sam Jones, the material having been provided by the chaired bard of the 1921 Caernarfon National Eisteddfod, Meuryn (R. J. Rowlands), and the producer being Wilbert Lloyd Roberts. Famous names that appeared on the programme included Cynan, Huw Jones, Charles Williams with the voices of Megan Lloyd George reading one of her father's speeches and Jubilee Young reciting a sermon by Christmas Evans.

It was an unforgettable night as far as my late wife and I were concerned. Every item was broadcast live on the radio, and the network 10 p.m. news from London had to be delayed until the end of the programme. We all fought back tears as we slowly queued to leave the Pavilion for the last time that night, but that which we witnessed to can never be erased. Nevertheless, we could all say with pride – I was there.

The Red Dragon Saga

Welsh people all over the world look forward to celebrating St David's Day, year after year, but few will know of a protest that caused a stir on 1 March, 82 years ago in Caernarfon Castle and spread through the whole of Wales. I was too young at the time to remember the incident and was given the details some years later by my parents.

The Wales of the 1930s was very different to the Wales of today and especially so in a garrison town such as Caernarfon, where the vast majority regarded themselves as being British first, despite the fact that the language of the home, the street and the shops was predominantly Welsh. All of us children in the elementary schools celebrated our patron saint's day with a concert in the morning and a half day's holiday in the afternoon. We wore a daffodil in our lapels and heard often the words 'Cymru am Byth' (Wales for Ever), but our heroes were always the Englishmen and Americans of the large screen. My father used to say that many of our compatriots only regarded themselves as Welsh for two weeks of the year, one being the first week in March in honour of St David and the other the first week in August when the National Eisteddfod was held. His name for them was: 'Cymry am Bythefnos' (Welsh for a fortnight).

This was typical of the era, but a Welsh awareness gradually emerged after the establishing of the Welsh Nationalist Party in Pwllheli in 1925 and the opening of their office in Caernarfon in 1930. In the beginning, although the membership was not large, these pioneers were instrumental in accomplishing invaluable work instilling a sense of pride in being Welsh into their fellow countrymen without tolerating unfair treatment of their nation.

It is this feeling of unfairness that was responsible for what happened on 1 March 1932. What reminded me of the protest was receiving a photo from Mr Keith Morris, local historian and webmaster of Caernarfon Traders. It was a photo of the tallest tower in Caernarfon Castle, the Eagle Tower, showing two flagpoles side by side. He wished to know the significance of the two poles. It was then that I remembered the story as I had heard it all those years ago from my parents. I then contacted Mrs Angharad Williams, Melin y Wig, Llys Gwyn, Caernarfon, as I knew that her father, the late Mr J. E. Jones, former general secretary of Plaid Cymru, had taken part in the act of protest at the Castle on St David's Day, 1932. In her father's book *Tros Gymru* (For Wales), (1970) he relates the full history of the incident in a chapter called 'Antur Tŵr yr Eryr' (The Eagle Tower Adventure).

On St David's Day 1931, he noticed that only the Union Jack had been hoisted on the Eagle Tower. Members of the Caernarfon Branch of the Welsh Nationalist Party (later to be named 'Plaid Cymru') felt strongly, as he did, that this was an insult to the Welsh nation and that it be brought to the attention of the authority responsible for the Castle.

As an organiser of the party, J. E. Jones wrote to the Member of Parliament for the constituency David Lloyd George, who was also Constable of the Castle and he forwarded the letter to the Minister for Buildings. Upon receiving a reply from an official of the Ministry, he sent it on to the Plaid Office. The reply was both unmannerly and insulting according

The second pole on the Eagle Tower

to J. E. Jones and he published it in the press. Many members of parliament from Wales asked questions on the matter in Westminster several times, seeking equal consideration be given to the hoisting of the Red Dragon. But the Minister, Mr Ormesby-Gore's reply was 'No', on each occasion, even to the last request on the day before to St David's Day 1932. This reply was also published in the press on 1 March, thus infuriating many Welsh people.

As a result four men decided on a course of direct action and at 10 a.m. on the following morning, J. E. Jones, dressed as a motor cyclist and carrying a rucksack, paid to go into the Castle and he was followed by three others: E. V. Stanley Jones, a young Caernarfon solicitor who pretended to be showing

J. E. Jones

two others around the castle. They were W. R. P. George, another solicitor and nephew of the famous David Lloyd George and Wil Roberts, a civil servant from Caernarfon. They went up the Eagle Tower, lowered the Union Jack and hoisted a very large Red Dragon. They then started to sing 'Land of my Fathers' and the people below in the town began to cheer on seeing the Red Dragon hoisted on the tallest tower in the Castle.

Eventually, the police were called and the four were escorted out of the Castle. The Red Dragon was lowered and the Union Jack rehoisted. After taking their names and addresses, the four involved were set free and no action was taken against them. In the minds of all who represented authority, the protest was over. But... there was more to come.

During the afternoon and without the knowledge of the morning's protesters, some 20 students from Bangor came to Caernarfon under the leadership of R. E. Jones, originally from Llangernyw, but remembered as a headteacher in Llanberis and a former Plaid Cymru parliamentary candidate for the Arfon constituency. They also paid for admission to the Castle and after taking a good look round they made for the Eagle Tower. They were surprised to find the main door to the tower locked, but fortunately they found a way in through an aperture in the wall and made their way up to the top. Once again the Union

Jack was lowered and the Red Dragon rehoisted. Police assistance was again requested and after some considerable deliberation the students were also escorted from the Castle. This time, however, one of them had succeeded to wrap the Union Jack around him under his clothes and took it straight to the Plaid Office.

Later R. E. Jones and others addressed a crowd that had gathered on Castle Square and some shouted for the Union Jack to be burned. It was fetched from the Plaid Office in haste and after unsuccessful attempts at burning it, it was decided that it be torn to pieces and many kept parts as souvenirs of the protest.

An exciting day! But it was not the end of the 'Adventure of the Eagle Tower' by a long way.

★ ★ ★ ★

The reaction to the protest caused embarrassment to the government of the day, both with pressure being put on it by Welsh members of parliament and the public at large throughout Wales. This must have resulted in a change of heart which can only be described as an U-turn. Shortly before St David's Day 1933, it was announced that the Red Dragon would be allowed to be hoisted side by side with the Union Jack on two occasions during the year, which were St David's Day and the monarch's birthday. This in effect meant that another flagpole had to be erected on the Eagle Tower.

It is not known what part the former premier David Lloyd George played in securing this concession, but it was he, as Constable, who was to the fore in the celebrations at the castle on 1 March 1933. In a special meeting of the town council, J. E. Jones and Nefydd Jones had argued strongly that a true nationalist should have the honour of taking part in the ceremony, but this was opposed vehemently and in his book *Tros Gymru*, J. E. states that E. P. Evans, county school headmaster, an enthusiastic Liberal and elder of Engedi Chapel, intimated that Lloyd George had given instructions that no-one but himself was to hoist the Red Dragon in the presence of the multitude. But, as it turned out, this was not the case.

In a local English-language newspaper, however, it was reported that the Mayor, Mr W. G. Williams, had the honour of hoisting the Red Dragon and the Deputy Constable of the Castle, Mr Charles A. Jones, a local solicitor and Magistrates' Clerk hoisted the Union Jack at 8 a.m. on the morning of 1 March. Many thousands of Welsh people visited the Castle during the morning and afternoon and they both sang and listened to local choirs singing patriotic songs. Lloyd George himself was said to have composed the words of one song and was very pleased with the rendering of it. It was 3 p.m. in the afternoon when

Lloyd George

he arrived at Caernarfon Station. There he was met
and taken to the Castle and dressed in his Constable's
attire.

He then addressed a crowd of over a thousand
people, which included a vast number of school
children. 'Unity' was the theme of the address by this
silver-tongued statesman on a historic St David's Day,
and all listened intently to every word uttered. His first
well-chosen words were: 'Mayor and Mayoress of this
ancient town of Caernarfon and fellow countrymen'
thus electrifying his audience to a warm response
and the children shouted 'Hooray'. He stated that he

had not come to Caernarfon that day to give them a speech, but to join with them in a celebration within the walls of the castle that was built to suppress the Welsh nation. On St David's Day, however, that which splits us such as party politics and sectarianism is forgotten and we are once again an united nation. He warmly welcomed this and compared it to the National Eisteddfod where all were of one accord and the differences on national matters such as education and religion were set aside for the duration of the festival. Such celebratory days were essential for the good of the nation.

He mentioned the Welsh language and quoted statistics that, if somewhat misleading, were designed to appeal to his captive audience. There were seven times as many people in Wales speaking the language as compared to the days of Llewelyn Fawr and Owain Glyndŵr and four times as many as in the days of Goronwy Owen. He then turned to the children and pointing to them said: 'and these will see to it that the language will be spoken for generations to come'. He then referred to the English language by saying that it was spoken by a third of the population of the world and for that reason: 'You people in Wales in learning both languages are on safe ground'.

He ended his address by stating how he had travelled from London to Caernarfon in seven hours that day and asked: 'What would the soldiers of Edward I, who guarded this castle, say if you were to tell them that? They would not believe it!' This was an attempt to explain how small the world had become in comparison with their day and he quoted an englyn by Robin Ddu Ddewin, an Angelsey poet, who lived 600 years earlier and who had prophesied that the time would come when men would fly.

The only reference to the previous year's protest was mentioned at the beginning of the speech when Lloyd George stated that he was not against battling. He himself had taken part in many battles in the past and would probably take part in many others. The crowd laughed and he went on to stress the purpose of the day's celebration which was 'Unity'.

The Mayor thanked him for the address, was seconded by the Deputy Constable of the Castle, Mr Charles A. Jones, and the meeting ended with the singing of both National Anthems, God Save the King and Hen Wlad Fy Nhadau.

In conclusion it would have been encouraging to state that the spirit of that particular St David's Day had remained, but that was not so. Not all buildings of importance saw fit to fly the Red Dragon on the day of the patron saint. Here is a translation of a quote from the Nationalist publication *Triban Rhyddid* in the year 1935:

Remember the Eagle Tower... But, it was the Union Jack that was flown from the Liberal Club in Caernarfon, even on St David's Day, although the Welsh Nationalist Party had specifically requested the hoisting of the Red Dragon.

Riot in 1752

On the south side of the altar at Llanbeblig Church, Caernarfon is a tablet inscribed with the words: 'S. M. William Williams, late of Glanrafon, Esq., His Majesty's Attorney General of North Wales. He died the 26th of April, 1769, aged 65. This monument was erected by his widow Hephzibah Williams.'

He lived at Plas Glanrafon, Castle Street, and in the book *Old Karnarvon* by W. H. Jones, published by H. Humphreys in 1882, the author refers to him as Councillor Williams and gives an account of a riot in the town in 1752. The authorities had heard a rumour that a large number of quarrymen from Mynydd y Cilgwyn and Rhostryfan intended raiding the granary in Shirehall Street, the reason being that the price of corn was purposely being kept high through legislation and ordinary people could not afford it. One morning in April 1752, being aware of the impending raid, Councillor Williams gathered together a number of men armed with guns, swords and bludgeons to defend the granary. In the meantime the insurgents had also made an emergency plan, should the authorities become aware of their intention. In south Penrallt, there lived an old man who earned his livelihood as an itinerant gelder and it

The Sportsman Hotel

was his practice, when looking for business, to stop at a crossroad or village square and blow his horn. This would alert the neighbourhood of his presence and any farmer requiring his services would go to him and accompany him to his farm. The quarrymen had made arrangements with the gelder to blow his horn should he believe them to be in danger.

At 10 a.m. the quarrymen marched into town and, by then the old man had heard that Councillor Williams and his men were waiting in the Sportsman Hotel in Castle Street, ready to pounce on the would-be raiders. The gelder then blew short blasts on his horn from his doorstep, which was directly opposite where Moriah Chapel later stood. The insurgents ran in the direction of Ty'n y Cei and waded across the river, making for Coed Helen, closely followed by

The Anglesey

the Councillor and his men. One quarryman, not easily frightened, was half-way across when he turned and said to his pursuers: 'You have no bullets, only powder in your guns.' The landlord of the Crown Inn replied by saying: 'I'll show you what I have in my gun,' and without hesitation shot him through the heart, killing him instantly. The insurgents rushed to retrieve his body and made haste in the direction of the woods. The Councillor and his supporters went in search of the old gelder and held a drumhead court-martial, before hanging him near the Anglesey tavern. The men took him down, placed him in a coffin and carried it to Llanbeblig cemetery. It was later said that he was still kicking as earth was thrown on the coffin.

In the meantime, the quarrymen had not been idle.

They had made a coffin for their comrade and had painted it, half in red and the other half, black. They then carried it through the streets of the town in a solemn procession and on to Llandwrog for burial.

There was, however, no end to the councillor's vindictiveness. He arranged for some of the insurgents to be brought before the Magistrates' Court and punished, and others were forced to flee the country. It was believed at the time that the ghost of the man in the red and black coffin haunted the Crown Inn for a century, right up to 1852 when the building was demolished to make way for the railway.

W. H. Jones, in his book, further states that the Exchequer Rolls of 1752 record the official version of what happened as follows: that two men in Caernarfon were hung for conspiracy – one of them being the old gelder and the other the quarryman who was killed – and the Councillor, His Majesty's Attorney General for North Wales, without doubt, had presented the case in this way to the authorities at headquarters.

The author, W. H. Jones, purposely omitted quoting the names of those who died, as descendants of the old gelder – respectable families – still resided in the town.

The Golden Age
of the Country Buses

Having bid farewell to the first decade of the millennium, it is difficult to imagine how transport developed over the previous century. The residents of Caernarfon and district seldom travelled in the horse-drawn buses of the 19th century and had to wait until 1909 before seeing a bus driven by a motor on their roads.

The first service bus carrying passengers in Caernarfonshire travelled between Caernarfon and Dinas Dinlle and it isn't difficult to imagine the excitement on witnessing this new device. Adults and children looked on in amazement on seeing a bus negotiating the streets without horses pulling it. Then, later on in the year, the bus was used to travel daily between Caernarfon and the village of Llanaelhaearn and on market day in Pwllheli it would continue on its journey to that town, returning late in the evening to Caernarfon.

This service was soon followed by other small companies. Between the years 1909 and the start of World War I in 1914, regular services ran from villages such as Rhostryfan, Nantlle and Penygroes to Caernarfon. When war broke out in 1914, however, it became more difficult to obtain supplies of petrol to run them and services were not allowed to run to villages where train services existed.

The speed of the earlier buses was between six and ten miles per hour and remained so throughout the War. But despite that more and more was learned about the effectiveness of motors during the War and many soldiers were taught to drive and to become mechanics. There are examples of many returning to civilian life and obtaining work as drivers of buses, vans and other vehicles. There were many opportunities for experienced drivers in the post-war years, with the result that many small companies were established.

These companies did not have fixed timetables, however, and could not be relied upon should a villager wish to catch a train for instance. The buses did not start until there were sufficient passengers to make the journey profitable, but despite this the public appreciated the service and, in general, the buses were reasonably full. It was also possible to use a bus to carry parcels and to do the work normally associated with the post office.

During the 1920s with scores of companies having been established, more than one company would travel on the same route and they were forced into adhering to a timetable so that buses belonging to different companies would not arrive at a bus stop at the same time, and this brought better organization to the services. By then, however, some companies had begun to call themselves according to the colour of their buses and some of the most popular in the area were Caernarfon red, Bangor blue and Bethesda grey, but not all of them. Others called their companies according to the name of the area they served, e.g. Peris Motors.

But there were others who were more ingenious. The owners of one company went under the initials UNU which was a form of abbreviating the English words You Need Us and another company in opposition decided to call their company INU (I Need You) This is a perfect example of the keen competition that existed among companies.

The rule was that every company should have a licence to serve between stipulated towns and villages and that they should not poach on other companies' territories. Therefore, should any company decide to

Buses on Castle Square, 1922

end its service in an area, it had a legal right to sell to another and, during the second quarter of 20th century, as many as 30 companies in north Wales sold out to the large English company, Crosville. However, some companies carried on and continue to serve their areas to this day.

Crosville established four centres in the county, one in each of the following places: Llandudno Junction, Bangor, Caernarfon and Pwllheli and ran their services from these centres. The one in Caernarfon was busy and had numerous employees in the form of drivers, conductors, ticket inspectors, mechanics, cleaners, managers and clerks.

Buses started on their various journeys from, and returned to, Castle Square and who can forget the crowds on the square on Saturday nights, half a century and more ago. Here is one personal recollection which happened sometime during the summer of 1949, when I, and two friends, stood near to where the Pound Stretcher Store is today. It was 9 p.m. on a Saturday night and we remained there watching the buses leave for their various destinations. We began counting how many left between 9 p.m. and 10.10 p.m., which was the time the last one departed. All the seats were full and many had standing-room only. We did not count how many were single and how many were double-deckers, but I can well remember how many buses we counted that night. There were 78.

Taking into consideration how full those buses were, I have no hesitation in stating that there must have been at least 50 persons to each bus. With this conservative estimate it makes a total of 3,900. Oh yes, it was the period following the end of World War II and the middle of the 20th century that can be termed the golden age of the country buses.

Villainy on Christmas Night

Christmas is associated with peace and joy, not with turmoil and sadness, with tenderness rather than violence. It is the season of goodwill. But this does not mean that the Devil is on holiday. Atrocities do happen even on Christmas Day itself, as the one that occurred in Holyhead on Christmas night 1909 proves.

A married woman, Gwen Ellen Jones from Bethesda, had been cohabiting with an Irish labourer named William Murphy, with whom she had a child. Murphy spent much time working away from home, but he regularly sent her maintenance money and a few days before Christmas 1909 he went to Gwen Ellen's father's home in Bethesda with a view to renewing their relationship. The old man told him she had gone to live on Anglesey, but he did not have her address.

Murphy eventually traced her to Holyhead and on Christmas night he approached her in a tavern and asked her to leave with him so that they could discuss their estranged situation. She left the Bardsey Island Inn with him of her own accord and that was the last time she was seen alive, apart from by those who saw and heard them both singing in each other's company whilst walking along the street.

What happened after they left the public house can only be imagined, but later that night Murphy went to the police station to confess to killing Gwen Ellen and he also led policemen to a ditch where her body was found. She had been strangled and her throat had been cut with a knife.

Murphy was arrested and, after a brief appearance at the Magistrates' Court in Holyhead on 27 December he was committed to stand trial at Beaumaris Assizes on 26 January 1910.

Even though the defence made a strong case in an attempt to prove to the jury that Murphy was not in his right mind when the offence occurred, the defendant was found guilty of murdering Gwen Ellen Jones on 25 December 1909. He was sentenced to death by hanging and spent the remainder of his days in Caernarfon Jail.

Many people were opposed to the death sentence and the solicitor, Mr William George, brother of David Lloyd George MP, organized a petition. It was signed by many influential persons and was sent to the Home Secretary. However, he decided not to intervene but to allow justice to take its course. Murphy's brother had to break the news to him. He showed no emotion and it is doubtful whether he had ever hoped for a favourable reply.

Father Gouzier, the Roman Catholic Prison Chaplain, who regularly attended to Murphy's spiritual needs, was of the opinion that he was very different from other prisoners he had known. Confirmation of his assessment is borne out by this story related to the author by the late Miss C. Limerick Jones, 12 Market Street, Caernarfon. Her grandfather, Richard Jones, pilot, lived in Shirehall Street and was sometimes employed at the Jail as an extra warder. He was with Murphy on the night before the execution and they talked together and played cards for hours. Shortly before 8 a.m. the prisoner shook Richard Jones by the hand and said: 'Thanks old man for everything'. He then walked as part of the procession to the scaffold. Henry Pierrpoint was the executioner assisted by John Ellis, who later became a public executioner.

The crowd eagerly awaited the hoisting of a black flag with its ominous message, but that did not happen, as the practice was discontinued in 1902, by an Act of Parliament. However, something unexpected did happen. The Church Bell of St Mary's began to toll, but stopped abruptly after striking only twice. Had the prisoner been reprieved? The sound of the trapdoor being opened was heard and everyone knew that it was not so. Later, it was learnt that the clapper of the church bell had worn thin and fallen, and that after 170 years of unbroken service.

★   ★   ★   ★

Whilst adapting the old jail for use as offices for the County Council in 1932, the bodies of William Murphy and two others executed at Caernarfon Jail were unearthed and permission was received from the Home Office to reinter them at the Llanbeblig Municipal Cemetery. That was done in the early hours of the morning, a short service took place, but those who buried him were not permitted to mark the location of the grave.

William Murphy

The clapper of the church bell

'Cyfrol sy'n ychwanegu
at hud hen dref arbennig iawn
mewn modd diddan a darllenadwy.'

Yr Athro Gwyn Thomas

Hanesion
Tre'r
Cofis

T Meirion Hughes

y Lolfa

£9.95

Looking for Wales
y Lolfa
An introductory guide
Gerald Morgan

£4.95

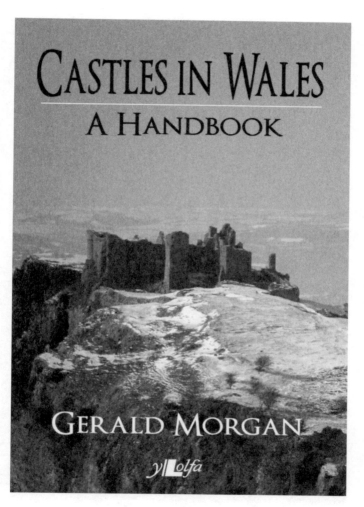

CASTLES IN WALES
A HANDBOOK

GERALD MORGAN

y Lolfa

£6.95

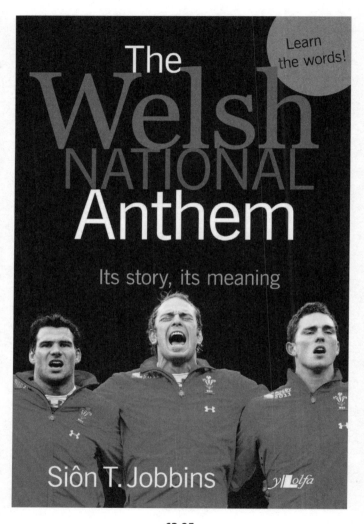

The Welsh NATIONAL Anthem

Its story, its meaning

Siôn T. Jobbins

£3.95

CASTLES
OF THE WELSH
PRINCES

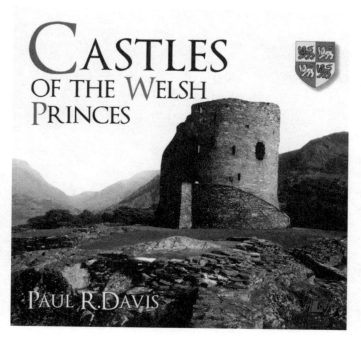

PAUL R. DAVIS

£7.95